Christmas Quilting Magic

Patterns to Spark Holiday Cheer

Table of Contents

- **Introduction** — 1
- **Tools & Materials** — 2
- **Basic Techniques** — 5
- **Patterns** — 15

  Little pine tree — 16

  Jolly Bars — 24

  Gnome Mini — 29

  Christmas Irish Chain — 38

  Oh Holly Night — 45

  Peppermint Mini — 52

  Square Panel Stars — 55

  Merry Stars — 61

  Winter Watch — 68

  Winter Tree — 75

- **Conclusion** — 81

Introduction

The holiday season is a time for joy, warmth, and creating memories that last a lifetime—and what better way to celebrate than through the art of quilting? **Christmas Quilting Magic: Patterns to Spark Holiday Cheer** invites you to bring festive beauty and heartfelt tradition into every stitch.

Inside these pages, you'll discover a collection of enchanting quilt patterns, from quick and cheerful projects to timeless heirloom pieces. Whether you are crafting cozy gifts for loved ones or decorating your home with handmade treasures, each design is meant to spark creativity, comfort, and holiday spirit.

Even if you're new to quilting, you'll find easy-to-follow instructions, helpful tips, and inspiration to make your sewing journey joyful and rewarding. Gather your favorite fabrics, thread your needle, and let's weave a little magic into this Christmas season—one beautiful quilt at a time.

Tools & Materials

1. Fabric Shears and Scissors

Every quilter needs at least one pair of large, high-quality fabric shears to use when cutting around templates or when they need to reach areas a rotary cutter can't.

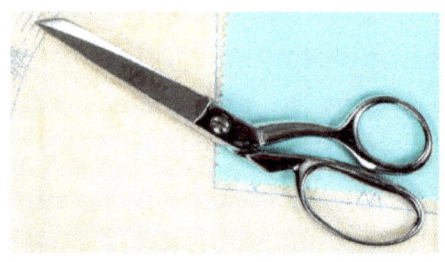

2. Rotary Cutters and Replacement Blades

Use a 45 mm or 60 mm rotary cutter 60 mm handles layers better, 45 mm offers more control. Keep spare blades for clean cuts and try decorative ones for fun edges.

3. Self-Healing Cutting Mats

A self-healing cutting mats give you years of service because your cuts won't leave indents on the surface.

4. Seam Rippers

A seam ripper is a basic tool for taking out stitches, and you'll use it again and again no matter what your skill level.

5. Acrylic Rulers

With their see-through material and easy-to-read markings, acrylic rulers make measuring a breeze so you can accurately cut your fabric.

6. Basic Sewing Machine and Feet

Many machines come with a special ¼" foot to make sewing a standard ¼" seam easier, but you can also learn to do it without this specialty foot.

7. Thread

Many quilters sew with 50-weight cotton or a poly-cotton blend of thread for basic piecing.

8. Pins and a Pincushion

Pins help quilters achieve accuracy in their piecing by keeping fabrics securely together for sewing. Choose sharp, sturdy sewing pins and use either a pin cushion or magnetic pin bowl to make them easy to store and use.

9. Clips

Not only are clips amazingly helpful for securing your binding, they're also a great alternative to pins when working with several layers of fabric.

10. Needles for Hand and Machine Sewing

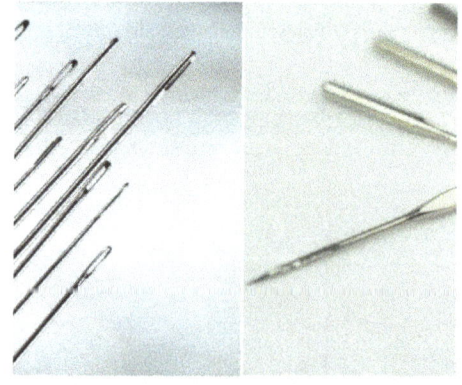

Keep extra machine and hand sewing needles. Machine needles break, and hand needles (like betweens, sharps, and straws) are great for binding, appliqué, and piecing. A needle threader helps with tiny eyes.

Basic Techniques

Cutting Fabrics

① Check the fabric grain (weaving direction).

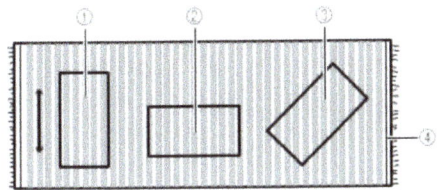

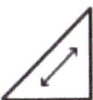

1 Lengthwise-grain fabric
2 Crosswise-grain fabric
③ Bias-grain fabric
4 Selvage

- When making pieces from patterned fabric, the pattern has priority over the fabric grain.
- Observe the fabric grain on the pattern if it is indicated.

② Align the lengthwise grain with the insertion direction.

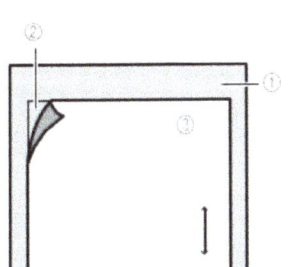

1 Standard mat
2 High tack adhesive fabric support sheet (An additional purchase may be required depending on the machine model.)
③ Wrong side of fabric

③ Select the patterns then arrange them

If the fabricgrain and pattern angle are not aligned, rotate the pattern.

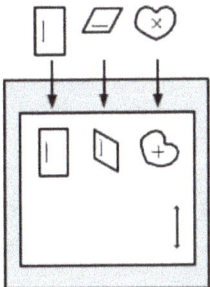

④ Specify the seam allowance.

Standard seam allowance

Patchwork	5 mm (3/16"), 1/4", 7 mm
Appliqué	3 mm (1/8"), 5 mm (3/16")

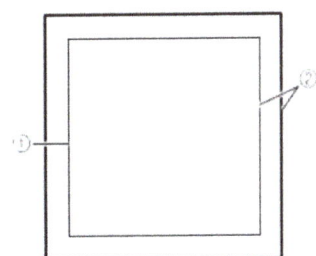

1 Stitching line
2 Seam allowance

Basic Hand Sewing Techniques

• Thread knot

Make a knot at the end of the thread to secure it.

1 Wind the thread 2 or 3 times around the needle

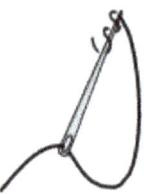

2 Hold the wound thread and pull out the needle.

1 Thread knot

3 Use scissors to cut off any excess thread

• Running stitch

Sew fine stitches when sewing pieces together.

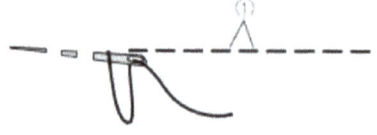

1 2 mm (1/16 inch)

• Blindstitch

Attach appliqués so that threads are imperceptible.

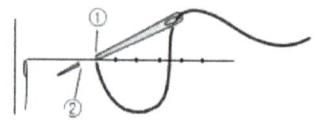

1 Insert the needle
2 Feed out the needle

• Backstitch

At the beginning and end of stitching, sew one backstitch, and then secure the thread to prevent it from becoming loose.

1 Feed out the needle
2 Insert the needle
③ Feed out the needle
4 Backstitch

- **French knot**

At the end of stitching, sew a backstitch, make a knot, and then cut the thread.

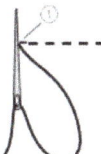 Place the needle at the end of stitching

1 Backstitch

 Wind the thread twice around the needle, hold the wound thread with your finger, and then pull out the needle.

- **Seam starting or ending point**

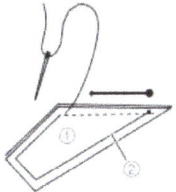 Sew the pieces together. At the beginning of stitching, make a knot in the thread, insert the needle in front of the stitching line, and then sew one backstitch

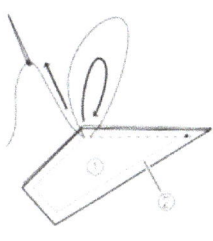

1 Wrong side of fabric
2 Stitching line

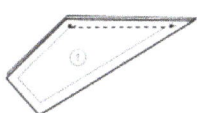 At the end of stitching, sew one backstitch, and then make a french knot at the corner

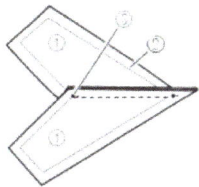

1 Wrong side of fabric
2 Stitching line
③ End point

- **Set in seam**

Continuously sew together multiple pieces of fabric by sewing each side without cutting the thread.

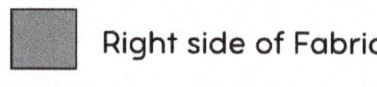 Right side of Fabric

 Wrong side of Fabric

① Sew pieces A' and B together. At the end point, pass the needle to the opposite side of A'

③ Overlap A and B, and then continue sewing.

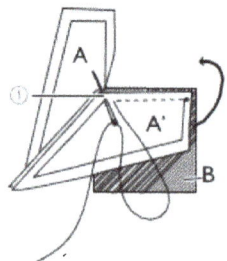

1 End point

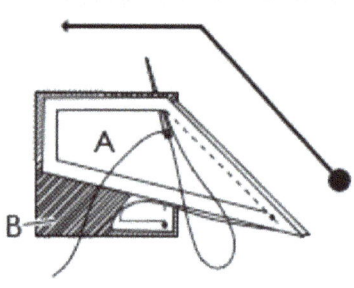

② Feed the needle out to the end point of A.

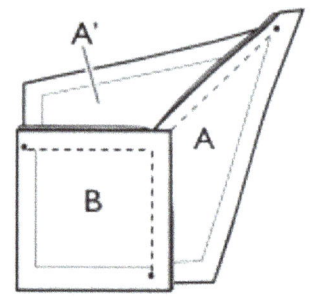

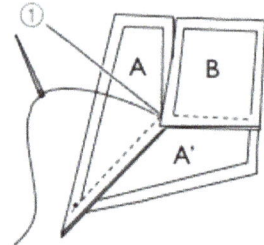

1 Start point

Sewing Pieces Together to Make the Top (Patchwork)

Using two types of fabric, prepare 4 squarepieces from one and 5 from the other.
Cut the pieceswith a seam allowance.

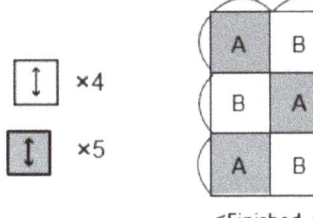

<Finished design>

- **Sewing order**

① Sew pieces together into rows

Fold over seam allowances in alternating directions

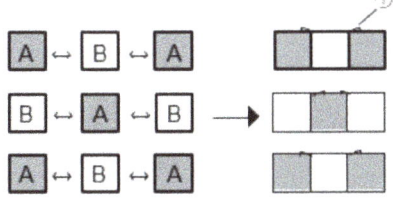

1 Seam allowance

② Sew the rows together to complete it

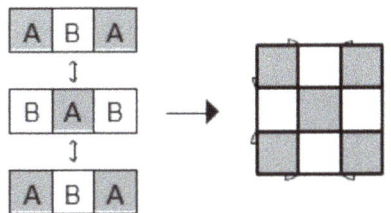

- **Sewing method**

① Align the pieceswith their right sides together, and then pin them.

At the beginning of stitching, insert the needle one stitch in front of the stitching line.

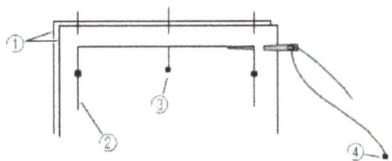

1 Right sides together
2 Stitching line
③ Pin
4 Thread knot

② Sew one backstitch, and then continuesewing a running stitch

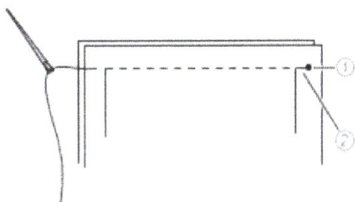

1 Thread knot
2 Backstitches

③ At the end of the stitching, sew one backstitch.

④ Make a French knot.

- **Sewing appliqué**

<Finished design>

1. Cut the appliqué pieces with a seam allowance applied

2. Make cuts 1 mm (1/16inch) from the stitching line

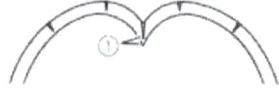

1 1 mm (1/16 inch)

Note

Make more cuts in tight curves.

3. Place the pattern on the appliqué piece, and then fold over the seam allowance using an iron or press

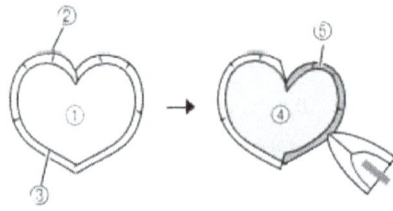

1 Wrong side of fabric
2 Cut
③ Stitching line
4 Pattern
5 Right side of fabric

4. Mark the base fabric

5. Remove the pattern, and then place the appliqué piece on the base fabric.

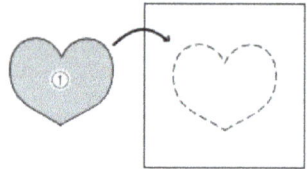

1 Right side of fabric

6. Attach the appliqué piece to the base fabric with blindstitching

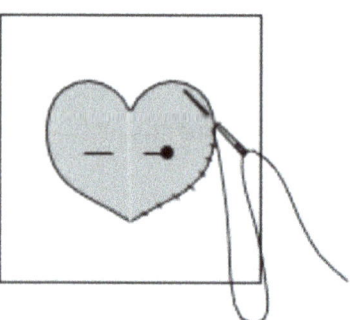

Basting

1 Prepare quilt battingand backing fabric 3 to 4 cm (1-3/16 to 1-9/16 inches) larger than the top, overlap the threelayers, and then secure them with pins.

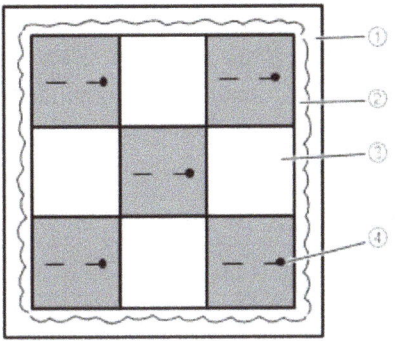

1 Wrong side of fabric
2 Quilt batting
③ Top
4 Pin

2 From the center to the outside, baste a grid pattern in the order shown in the illustration. At the beginning of stitching, make a thread knot. At the end of stitching, sew a backstitch, and then cut the thread

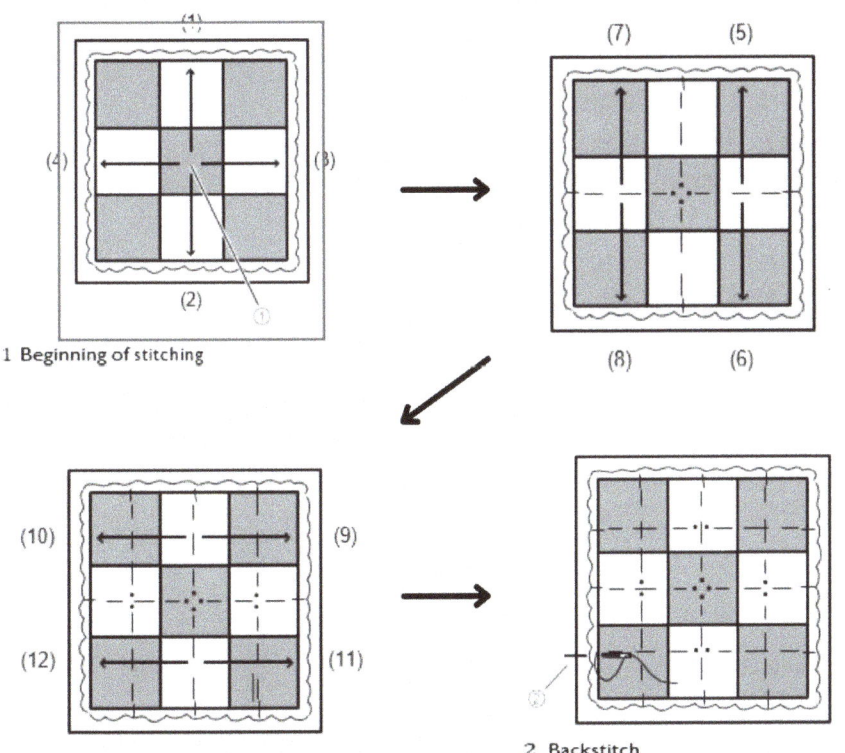

1 Beginning of stitching

2 Backstitch

Quilting

- **Quilting order**

From the center to the outside, sew symmetrically in the order shown in the illustration.

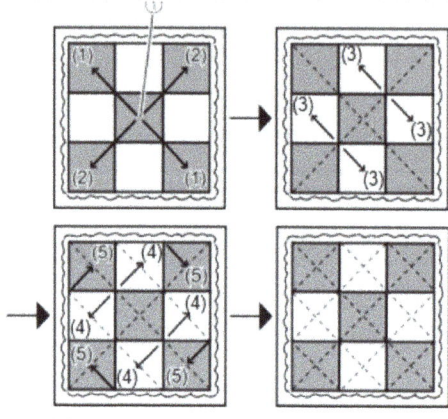

1 Beginning of stitching

- **Beginnging of Quilting**

1 Insert the needle slightly away from the starting point and pull the thread so the knot is hidden between the top fabric and the backing.

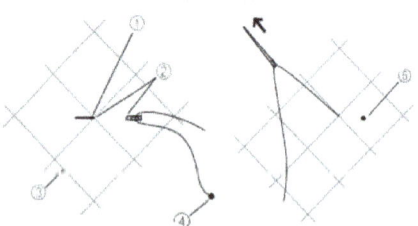

① Start of quilting
② 2 to 3 cm (3/4 to 1-3/16 inches)
③ Quilting lines
④ Thread knot
⑤ The thread knot is inside.

2 At the beginning of stitching, sew one backstitch

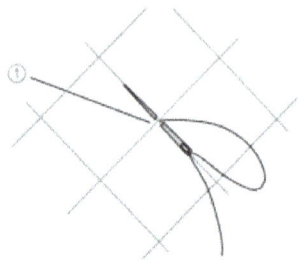

- **Ending stitching**

1 Backstitch, make a French knot, then reinsert the needle to hide the knot between layers.

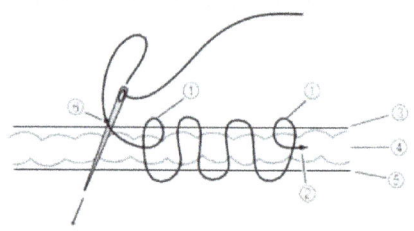

1 Backstitches
2 Thread knot
③ Top
4 Quilt batting
5 Back of fabric
6 French knot

2 Trim backing and batting, leaving a 7 mm (1/4 inch) edge for bias tape.

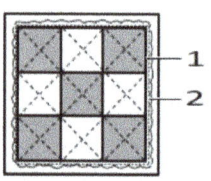

1 Top (patchwork)
2 Cut off, leaving for the bias tape a finished width from the edge of the top.

Binding (Finishing FabricEdges)

• Making bias tape

1. Make bias tape with a finished width of 7 mm

2. Draw a 35-mm-wide strip at a 45° angle on the fabric, and then cut it out.

3. Draw a line 7 mm from the edge of the bias tape.

4. Sew the stripstogether to a length of 15 to 20 cm (6 to 8 inches) plus the length of the four sides of the quilt.

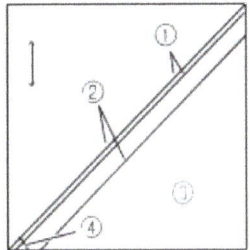

1) 7 mm (1/4 inch)
2) 35 mm (1-3/8 inches)
3) Wrong side of fabric
4) 45°

• Connecting bias tape sections

With their right sides together, align the ends of two sections, and then sew them together with 7 mm (1/4 inch) seam allowance

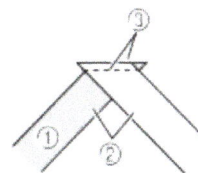

1) Right side of fabric
2) 1 Right sides together
3) 7 mm (1/4inch)

• Binding

1. Align the 7 mm (1/4 inch) line with the stitching line of the quilt, and then sew. Fold over 1 cm (3/8 inch) of the end of the bias tape

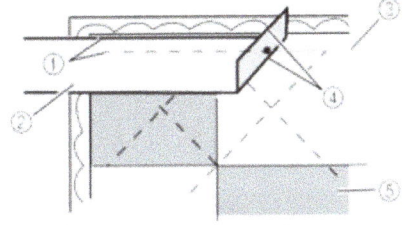

1) 7 mm (1/4inch)
2) Wrong side of fabric
3) Stitching line
4) 4 Fold over 1 cm (3/8 inch).
5) Right side of quilt

2. At the corner,fold the bias tape out at a 45° angle

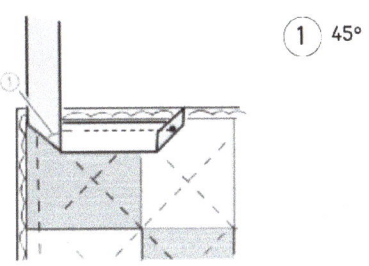

1) 45°

3. Fold it at a 90° angle, and then sew along the 7 mm (1/4 inch) line.

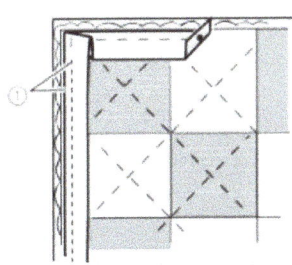

4 Sew all along the edges and return to the folded back end of the bias tape. Cut off any excess bias tape

(1) Overlap the fold.

(2) Excess bias tape

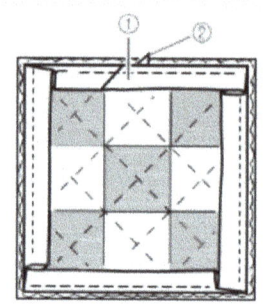

5 Turn the quilt over, cover the seam allowance with the bias tape, and then finish it with blindstitching.
The cornerwill be mitered as shown in the illustration.

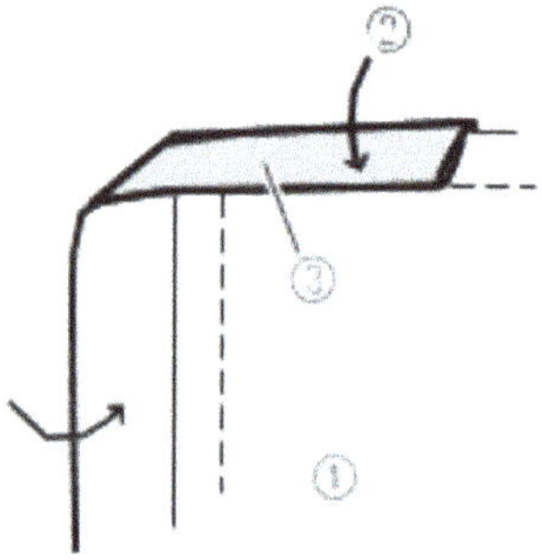

(1) Wrong side of Fabric
(2) Fold in three
(3) Right side of bias tape

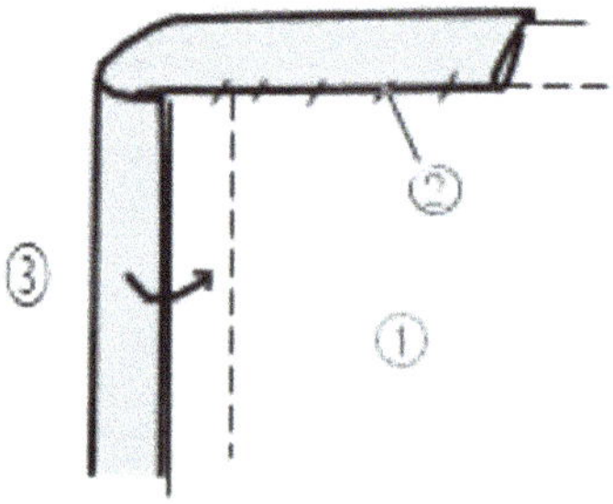

(1) Wrong side of Fabric
(2) Blindstitch
(3) Fold in three

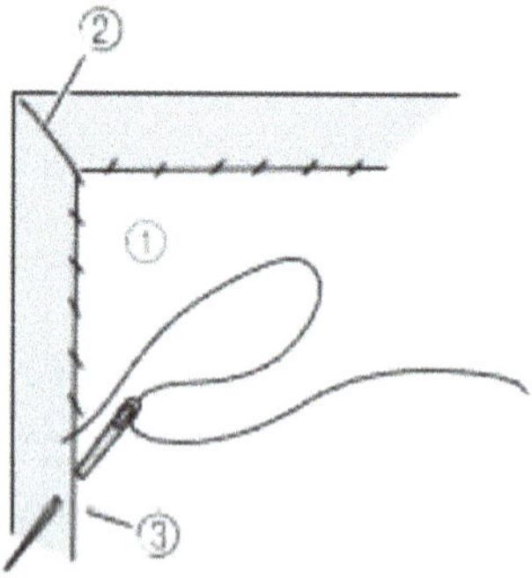

(1) Wrong side of Fabric
(2) Mitered
(3) Blindstitch

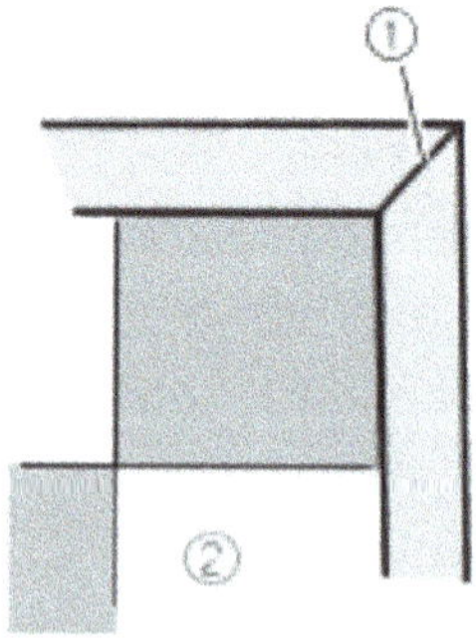

(1) Mitered
(2) Right side of quilt

Patterns

 Little pine tree 16

 Jolly Bars 24

 Gnome Mini 29

 Christmas Irish Chain 38

 Oh Holly Night 45

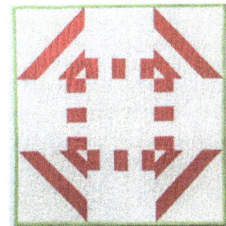 Peppermint Mini 52

 Square Panel Stars 55

 Merry Stars 61

 Winter Watch 68

 Winter Tree 75

Little Pine Trees Quilt

Materials

To make this 53" x 51" throw-sized Pine Trees Quilt, you will need

- 2 1/2 yards of cream or white fabric for the background
- 6 squares 10"x10" of different green print fabrics for the green trees
- 1 red print square 10" x 10" for the red trees
- 1/8 yard brown fabric for the trunks
- 1/2 yard of fabric for the binding
- 3-4 yards of fabric for the quilt back

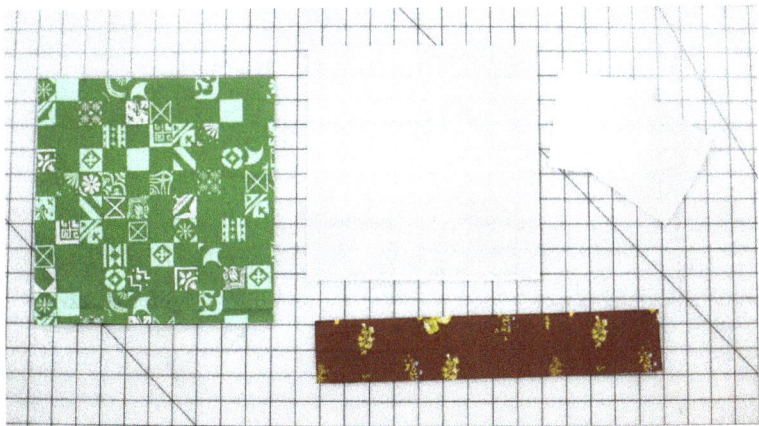

Instructions

- **Cutting Instructions**

To make the blocks, you will need:

- 7 white or cream squares 9 1/2" x 9 1/2"
- 13 white squares 4" x 4"
- 7 brown strips 2 1/2" x 14"

This is in addition to the 7 print squares listed above.

For the sashing and borders, cut the following from white/cream fabric:

- 32 strips 2 1/2" x 9 1/2"
- 24 squares 2 1/2" x 2 1/2"
- 2 squares 13 7/8" x 13 7/8"
- 2 squares 7 1/4" x 7 1/4"
- 2 strips 2 1/2" x 47" (side borders)
- 1 strip 2 1/2" x 51" (bottom border)
- 1 strip 4 1/2" x 51" (top border)

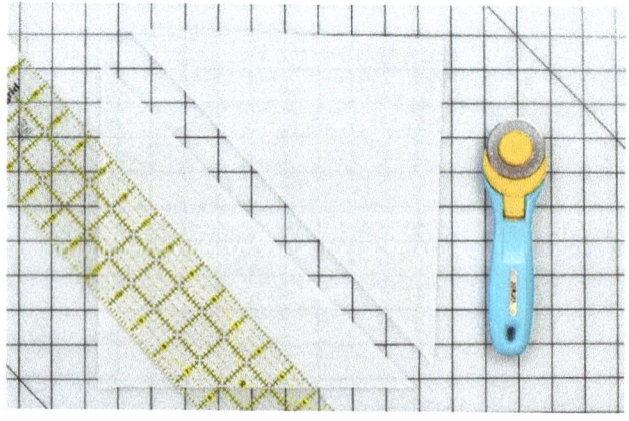

- **Make 7 Trunk Pieces**

All seam allowances on this quilt are 1/4".

1. 'Slash' each 9 1/2" white or cream square in half diagonally.

2. Fold each of the triangle pieces in half and mark the center of the long edge

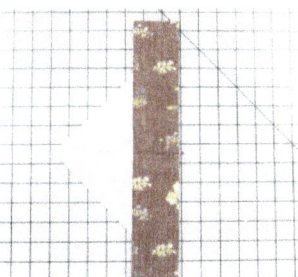

3. Lay a brown strip along the long edge of a triangle, matching the center marks. Stitch. Press the seam toward the darker fabric.

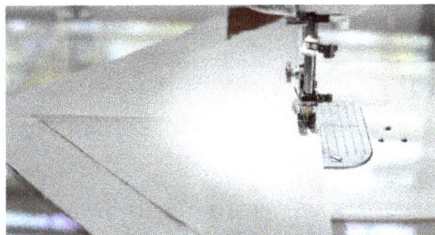

4. Lay the second triangle along the other edge of the brown strip, matching the center marks. Stitch. Press the seam toward the darker fabric

Repeat to make 7 trunk pieces.

- **Use the Half Square Triangle Method to make Tree Blocks**

1. Use a fabric pen and ruler to draw a diagonal line on the back of each 10" print square.

   Then draw a line on either side of the center line, 1/4" away from the center line.

2. Center a print square on top of a trunk piece and pin them right sides together.

3. Stitch along both of the outer marked lines

4. Cut the block in half along the center marked line.

5. Trim each block to 9½", keeping the diagonal seam centered. Repeat 6 more times to make 14 blocks

6. Use the fabric marking pen to draw a diagonal line down the center of each 4" square piece.

7. Stitch along the diagonal line. Trim away the corner 1/4" past the stitching. Press flat.
   Repeat to make 11 green tree blocks and 2 red tree blocks. You will have 1 green tree block leftover

- **Add the Quilt Sashing**

1. Arrange the 13 tree blocks in the pattern above.

2. Sew a 2½" x 9½" sashing strip to the right of each block, join blocks into diagonal rows, then add a sashing strip to each row's end.

3. Cut the two 13⅞" squares into 8 triangles and sew them to the ends of the 4 shorter rows, matching their positions carefully.

4. Cut the two 7 1/4" squares in half diagonally to get 4 triangles total (2 from each square).

   Sew two half square triangle pieces to the ends of the longest row as seen above.

   Set aside the 2 remaining pieces for later.

5 Make sashing strips to sew in between the diagonal rows. Using 2 1/2" squares in between 9 1/2" strips will help you line up each row perfectly.

Sew:
- 2 rows with 1 sashing strip and 2 squares
- 2 rows with 3 sashing strips and 4 squares
- 2 rows with 5 sashing strips and 6 squares

6 Sew the sashing strips in between the diagonal rows.

7 Sew the last two half square triangles to the remaining corners.

8 Trim away the corners of the sashing squares that stick out to make the sides of the quilt top straight in preparation for the borders.

- **Add Quilt Borders**

1. Sew 2 1/2" wide border strips to the sides of the quilt top.

2. Sew a 2 1/2" wide border strip to the bottom of the quilt.

3. Sew a 4 1/2" wide border strip to the top of the quilt – this wider strip creates an illusion to make the trees seem centered.

Jolly Bar Quilt Pattern

Materials

- Two Windermere Jolly Bars or sixty-four 5" x 10" rectangles (Fabric A)
- 2 1/2 yards solid (18606-21)
- 3/4 yard binding (18610-16)
- 5 1/8 yards backing (18610-13)

Cut solid fabric into:
- 32 – 9 1/2" x 10" rectangles (Fabric B)

Cut binding fabric into:
- 8 – 2 ½" x width of fabric strips (Fabric C)

Finished Size: 63 ½" x 81 ½"

Instructions

- **Block Assembly**

Use 1/4" seams and press as arrows indicate throughout

1. Assemble two Fabric A rectangles.
   - Rectangle Unit should measure 9 1/2" x 10".
   - Make thirty-two.

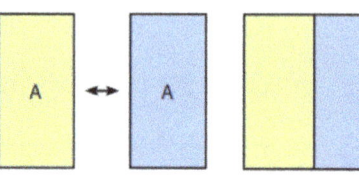

Make thirty-two.

2. With right sides facing, layer a Fabric B rectangle with a Rectangle Unit.
   - Pay close attention to unit placement.
   - Stitch ¼" away from the edge on the top and bottom.
   - Layered Unit should measure 9 1/2" x 10".
   - Make thirty-two.

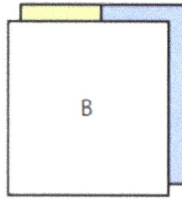

Make thirty-two.

3. Cut the Layered Unit in half across the width.
   - No Bake Block should measure 9 1/2" x 9 1/2".
   - Make sixty-four.
   - You will not use one No Bake Block.

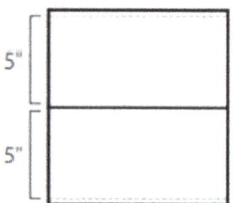
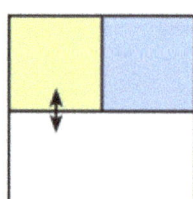
Make sixty-four.

- **Quilt Rows**

  ① Assemble seven No Bake Blocks.
  - Pay close attention to block placement.
  - Row One should measure 9 1/2" x 63 1/2".
  - Make five.

  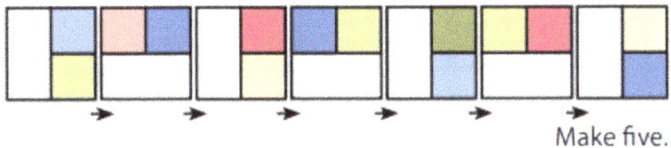
  Make five.

  ② Assemble seven No Bake Blocks.
  - Pay close attention to block placement.
  - Row Two should measure 9 1/2" x 63 1/2".
  - Make four.

  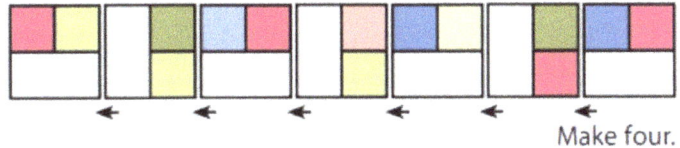
  Make four.

- **Quilt Center**

  Assemble the Quilt Center.

  Quilt Center should measure 63 1/2" x 81 1/2"

- **Finishing**

1. Piece the Fabric C strips end to end for binding.

2. Quilt and bind as desired.

Gnome Mini Quilt

Materials

To make the 33" quilt above, you will need:

- a fat quarter each of red, blue, green, and white fabric
- 1/2 yard of cream fabric
- a scrap each of brown and skin color fabric
- a 3" square of fusible web for applique
- 37" square of batting
- 1 yard plus 1" of backing fabric
- 1/3 yd binding fabric

Intructions

- ## Cutting

Cut the following patches for each 12" Gnome Quilt Block:

From the cream fabric, cut:
- 2 squares 6 1/2" x 6 1/2"
- 2 squares 2 1/2" x 2 1/2"

From the blue fabric, cut:
- 1 rectangle 6 1/2" x 12 1/2"

From the white fabric, cut:
- 1 rectangle 4 1/2" x 8 1/2"

From the red fabric, cut:
- 2 rectangles 2 1/2" x 4 1/2"
- 2 squares 4 1/2" x 4 1/2"
- 1 rectangle 2 1/2" x 12 1/2"

For the nose applique:
- Trace the nose template Cut along the traced line and set aside.

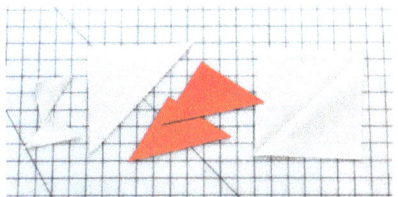

Cutting Instructions for one 12" (finished) Pine Tree Block:

From the green fabric, cut:
- 3 squares 3 1/2" x 3 1/2"
- 1 rectangle 3" x 2 1/2"
- 1 rectangle 3" x 3 1/2"
- 1 rectangle 3" x 4 1/2"
- 1 rectangle 3" x 5 1/2"

From the green fabric, cut:
- 1 square 2 1/2" x 2 1/2"

From the cream fabric, cut:
- 4 squares 3" x 3"
- 3 squares 3 1/2" x 3 1/2"
- 2 rectangles 3" x 4"
- 2 rectangles 3" x 2 1/2"
- 2 rectangles 3" x 2"
- 2 rectangles 2 1/2" x 5 1/2"

For the sashing, cut:
- 4 strips 3 1/2" x 12 1/2"
- 1 square 3 1/2" x 3 1/2"

For the borders, cut:
- 2 strips 3 1/2" x 27 1/2"
- 2 strips 3 1/2" x 33 1/2"

- **Make Flying Geese Units (Gnome Quilt)**

1. Mark a diagonal line on all of the square pieces (6in all)

2. To make the hat flying geese unit, place one of the 6 1/2" squares on top of the 6 1/2" x 12 1/2" blue piece, right sides together as seen above.

3. Stitch along the crease or marked line.

4. Trim away the fabric 1/4" past the sewn line. Open the piece and press flat.

5. Place the remaining 6 1/2" square on the other side of the flying geese unit as seen above. Pin along the line.

6. Stitch along the line.

7. Trim away the extra fabric 1/4" past the line of stitching, open, and press as before.

8. Follow steps 2-7 above with the 4 1/2" red squares and 4 1/2" x 8 1/2" white rectangle to make a flying geese unit for the beard.

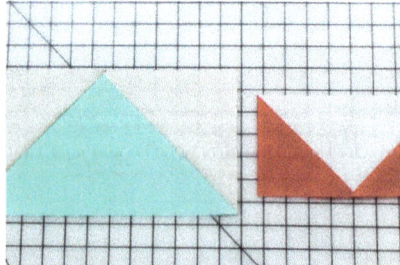

Use the 'Snowball Corner Method' to make the gnome bottom:

1. Pin the 2 1/2" cream colored squares to the ends of the 2 1/2" x 12 1/2" rectangle, right sides together.

2. Stitch across the creased or marked line.

3. Trim away the extra fabric 1/4" past the line.

4. Press the triangles open.

Assemble the Block:

1. Sew the red 2 1/2" x 4 1/2" rectangles to the sides of the red and white flying geese unit.

2. Arrange the block in three rows as seen above. Stitch together.

3. Remove the paper backing from the nose applique piece. Press to fuse it in the center of the block

4. Sew the nose to the block using your desired appliqué stitch.

- **Make Flying Geese Units (Pine Tree)**

1. Mark a diagonal line on 2 of the 3" square cream pieces

2. Place one of the 3" squares on top of the 3" x 5 1/2" green piece, right sides together. Pin along the line.

3. Stitch along the crease or marked line.

4. Trim away the fabric 1/4" past the sewn line

   Open the piece and press flat.

5. Place the remaining 3" square on the other side of the flying geese unit. Pin along the line.

6. Stitch along the line.

7. Trim away the extra fabric 1/4" past the line of stitching, open, and press as before.

Make 6 cream and green Half Square Triangle units:

1. Fold the three 3 1/2" squares in half diagonally and press to make a crease or draw a line with a pencil or fabric marking pen.

2. Place the 3 squares right sides together with the 3 green squares of the same size and pin.

3. Sew each square twice: once on either side of the line, 1/4" away from the line.

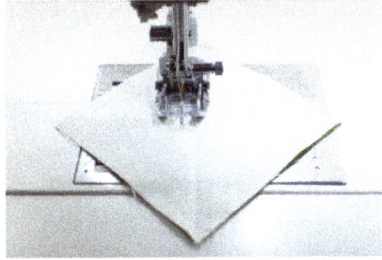

4. Cut the squares in half along the marked line. Open and press each square flat.

5. Trim the half square triangles so they are each exactly 3" square.

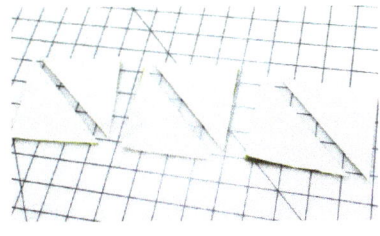

Assemble the Pine Tree Quilt Block

1. Sew the flying geese unit together with the two 3" x 4" cream rectangles

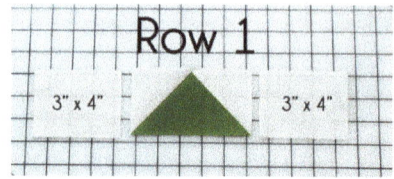

2. Sew together the two remaining cream 3" squares, two HST's, and the green 3" x 2 1/2" rectangle

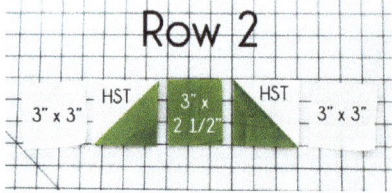

3. Sew together the two cream 3" x 2 1/2" rectangles, two HST's, and the green 3" x 3 1/2" rectangle

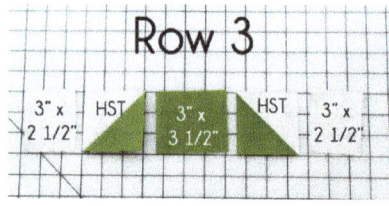

4. Sew together the two cream 3" x 2" rectangles, two HST's, and the green 3" x 4 1/2" rectangle

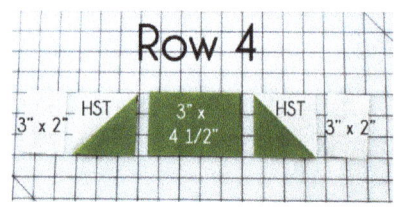

5. Sew together the two cream 2 1/2" x 5 1/2" rectangles and the brown 2 1/2" square

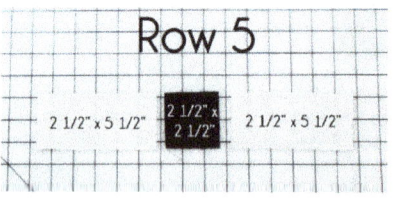

6. Press the seams and sew the 5 rows together.

- **Assembly**

1. Sew a gnome block and a tree block together with a sashing strip in between them.

2. Sew the other tree block and gnome block together in the opposite order – also with a sashing strip in between them.

3. Sew the last two sashing strips together with the 3 1/2" square in between them.

4. Sew the 3 pieces together.

5. Sew the 3 1/2" x 27 1/2" border strips to the sides of the quilt top.

6. Sew the 3 1/2" x 33 1/2" border strips to the top and bottom of the quilt top.

7. Sandwich, baste, quilt, and bind as desired!

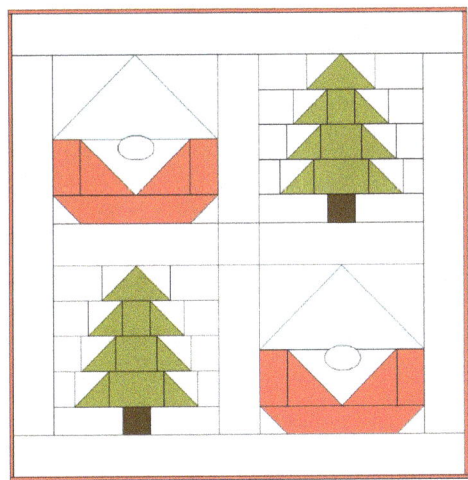

Christmas Irish Chain Quilt

Materials

To making the 77" x 77" quilt, you will need:

- 1 yard of dark green fabric
- 1 yard of light green fabric
- 1 yard of dark red fabric
- 1 yard of light red fabric
- 1/4 yard more of light red fabric for the sashing and Holly Block centers
- 1/4 yard yellow/gold fabric
- 3 1/2 yards of cream or white background fabric
- 5 yards of backing fabric
- 3/4 yards for the binding
- a piece of batting at least 81" x 81"

Intructions

• Cutting Instructions for Single Blocks

For one Holly Block (13" finished), cut:

- 4 dark green strips 2 1/2" x 4 1/2"
- 4 light green strips 2 1/2" x 4 1/2"
- 2 dark green strips 2 1/2" x 6 1/2"
- 2 light green strips 2 1/2" x 6 1/2"
- 8 background fabric squares 2 1/2" x 2 1/2"
- 4 background fabric strips 2 1/2" x 6"
- 1 light red square 2 1/2" x 2 1/2"

For one Poinsettia Block (13" finished), cut:

- 2 dark red squares 6" x 6"
- 2 light red squares 6" x 6"
- 8 background fabric squares 2" x 2"
- 4 yellow/gold squares 2" x 2"
- 2 background color strips 2" x 10 1/2"
- 2 background color strips 2" x 13 1/2"

Cutting Instructions for a 77" x 77" Quilt

From the dark green fabric:
- 52 strips 2 1/2" x 4 1/2"
- 26 strips 2 1/2" x 6 1/2"

From the dark red fabric
- 24 squares 6" x 6"

From the light red fabric
- 24 squares 6" x 6"
- 49 squares 2 1/2" x 2 1/2"

From the binding fabric cut:
- 8 strips 2 1/2" x width of fabric

From the light green fabric:
- 52 strips 2 1/2" x 4 1/2"
- 26 strips 2 1/2" x 6 1/2"

From the yellow/gold fabric
- 48 squares 2" x 2"

From the background fabric
- 24 strips 2" x 10 1/2"*
- 24 strips 2" x 13 1/2"*
- 60 strips 2 1/2" x 13 1/2"
- 96 squares 2" x 2"
- 104 squares 2 1/2" x 2 1/2"
- 52 strips 2 1/2" x 6"

- **Sew the Holly Blocks**

Make 13 for the entire quilt. Use a scant 1/4" seam allowance for best results.

1. Sew a 2 1/2" background fabric square to each 2 1/2" x 4 1/2" light green and dark green strip.

2. Sew two dark green + background fabric units to a 2 1/2" x 6 1/2" light green fabric strip.

3. Sew two light green + background fabric units to a 2 1/2" x 6 1/2" dark green fabric strip.

4. Cut each unit in half diagonally, cutting through the strips.

5. Sew one dark/ light/ dark triangle to one light/ dark/ light triangle to make a holly unit.

6. Sew two holly units to either side of a 2 1/2" x 6" background fabric strip

7. Sew two 2 1/2" x 6" background fabric strips to either side of a 2 1/2" x 2 1/2" light red square

8. Sew two holly pieces to either side of a red and cream piece. Repeat to make 13 blocks for the large quilt.

- **Sew the Poinsettia Blocks**

Make light and dark red half square triangle (HST) units:

① Place each light red square right sides together with a dark red 6" x 6" square and pin together.

② Sew diagonally across each piece twice, a scant 1/4" on either side of the drawn line.

③ Cut each piece in half diagonally along the drawn line. Open and press the seam toward the darker fabric. Trim each HST unit to 5 1/2" square.

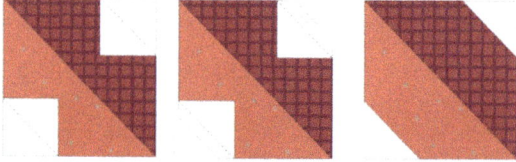

Add 'snowball corners':

① Place a 2" background fabric square against the two plain fabric corners of a HST unit

② Stitch across each 2" square diagonally. Trim away the extra fabric 1/4" past the stitching.

③ Open the corner and press. Press one seam toward the dark red fabric and the other (light red) seam toward the corner.

④ Place a 2" yellow/gold fabric square against the lower right corner of the HST unit

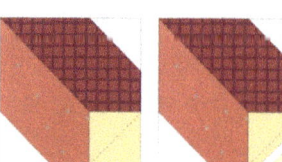 

5. Stitch across each 2" square diagonally as seen above (right on top of the line, if you drew one). Trim away the extra fabric 1/4" past the stitching.

6. Open the corner and press. Press the seam open or to one side.

7. Sew two HST units together left. Press the seam toward the darker fabric. Repeat to make 2 units for one block or 24 units for 12 blocks.

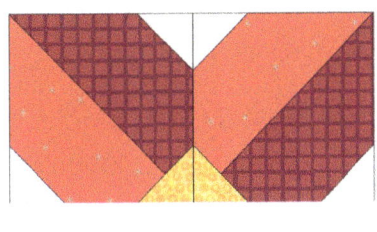

8. Sew 2 units together to make a flower. Repeat to make 12 flowers if you are making a large quilt.

9. Sew two 2" x 10 1/2" background fabric strips to the sides of each flower. Press the seams as desired.

10. Sew the two 2" x 13 1/2" background fabric strips to the top and bottom edges of each flower. Press the seams as desired

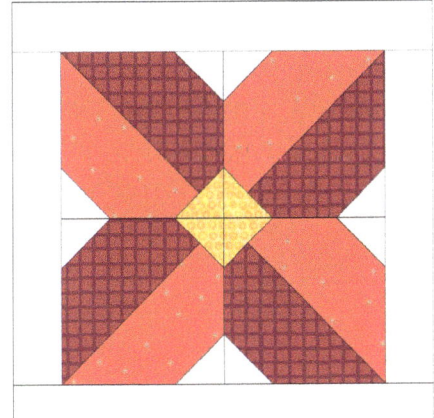

- **Assemble the Large Quilt**

Make 13 for the entire quilt. Use a scant 1/4" seam allowance for best results.

1. Sew 3 Holly Blocks and 2 Poinsettia Blocks in a row with 2½" x 13½" sashing strips between and on each end, pressing seams toward the sashing. Repeat to make 3 rows.

2. Sew 2 Holly Blocks and 3 Poinsettia Blocks in a row with 2½" x 13½" sashing strips between and on each end, pressing seams toward the sashing. Repeat to make 2 rows.

3. Sew 5 sashing strips with 2½" x 2½" light red squares between and on each end, pressing seams toward the sashing. Repeat to make 6 sashing rows.

4. Sew the rows of quilt blocks and the sashing rows together in an alternating pattern. Press the seams toward the sashing.

Oh Holy Night Quilt

Materials

- 1 1/4 yards of dark background fabric (40-42" wide)
- 1/4 yard of gold fabric for the star (if your fabric is directional, you'll need a fat quarter or 1/2 yard)
- 1/4 yard of white fabric for the star and appliqué letter (a FQ is fine)
- double sided fusible web for applique fabric marking pen or pencil

To finish the quilt, you will need:

- 1 1/8 yards of backing fabric
- 3/8 yards for the binding
- a piece of batting at least 41" x 41"

Instructions

Cutting

From the background fabric, cut:
- 1 rectangle 8 1/2" x 36"
- 1 rectangle 4 1/2" x 36 1/2"
- 1 rectangle 24 1/2" x 18 1/2"
- 1 rectangle 24 1/2" x 6 1/2"
- 2 rectangles 15 1/2 x 6 1/2" (for use with template A)
- 2 rectangles 3 1/2" x 6 1/2" (for use with template B)
- 4 squares 3 1/2" x 3 1/2" (for use with template C)

From the gold star fabric, cut:
- 1 rectangle 15 1/2" x 3 1/2" (for use with template D)
- 7 squares 3 1/2" x 3 1/2" (for use with template E)

From the white fabric, cut:
- 4 squares 3 1/2" x 3 1/2"

From the binding fabric cut:
- 4 strips 2 1/2" x width of fabric

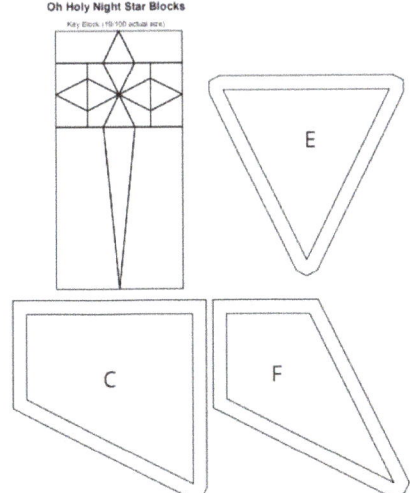

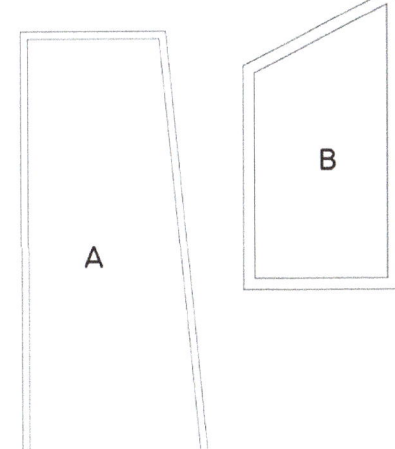

How to Cut the Quilt Block Shapes

1. Place the two 15 1/2" x 6 1/2" rectangles right sides together and lay template A on top.

2. Place the two 3 1/2" x 6 1/2" rectangles right sides together and lay template B on top.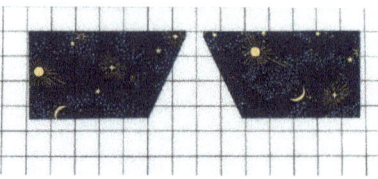

3. Place two 3 1/2" x 3 1/2" background fabric squares right sides together and lay template C on top.

4. Use the same technique and the seven 3 1/2" gold fabric squares to cut 7 from template E.

5. Cut a long triangle using the 15 1/2" x 3" gold fabric piece and template D.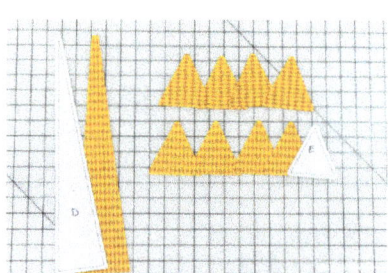

6. Use template F to cut 4 shapes from the white 3 1/2" squares.

7. Use small sharp scissors to cut out each letter along the lines. Cut out the negative spaces within the letters, as required too.

- ## Sew the Star Block

1. Begin with the 4 white pieces cut from template F and 4 of the gold pieces cut from template E.

2. Place a white piece on top of a gold piece as shown above left. Stitch with a 1/4" seam allowance.

3. Place two adjacent pieces together and stitch with a 1/4" seam allowance.

4. Place the two halves together and stitch.

5. The top row of the star block uses one triangle from template F and the two pieces cut from template B.

6. Sew together two pieces cut from template C and one triangle cut from template F to make a side unit. Press the seams open.

7. The bottom row of the star requires the two pieces cut from template A and the gold triangle cut from template D.

Finish Sewing the Christmas Star Quilt

1. Sew the 24 1/2" x 6" background fabric rectangle to the right side of the star block.

2. Sew the 24 1/2" x 18 1/2" background fabric rectangle to the left side of the star block.

3. Sew the 4 1/2" x 36 1/2" background fabric rectangle to the top of the quilt.

4. Sew the 8 1/2" x 36 1/2" background fabric rectangle to the bottom of the quilt.

- ## Sandwich and Quilt the quilt

1. Cut a piece of backing fabric in at least 41" x 41".

2. Sandwich the quilt top, batting, and backing together and baste.

3. Quilt the quilt top as desired.

- ## Applique the Words 'Oh Holy Night...'

1. Mark two lines to help with letter placement.

2. Place the letter 'h' from the word 'night' over the vertical line, with the bottom of the letter on the horizontal line.

3. Remove the paper backing from the letters. Press gently to adhere them to the quilt.

4. Sew around each letter with a straight stitch, satin stitch, or other appliqué stitch.

- ## Trim and Bind

1. Trim away the extra batting and backing and make your quilt square.

2. Cut 4 strips of binding 2 1/2" x width-of-fabric (or as desired) and sew them together using diagonal seams. Bind the quilt using your preferred method.

Peppermint Mini Quilt

Materials

- 1/2 Yard for the Red
- 1/2 Yard Solid White or White Print for the HSTs and Inner Square
- 1 Yard for the Backing and Binding
- 22 1/2" x 22 1/2" Piece of Batting
- Coordinating Thread for Piecing and Quilting
- Foundation Paper Piece Pattern
- General Sewing Supplies

Instructions

- ## Cutting

1. Cut (1) 7 1/2" x 7 1/2" solid white square for the center block.

2. Pre-cut the solid red and white fabric into 2 1/2" wide strips to use for the peppermint stripes.

   - 2 squares 9" x 9" that I cut diagonally to make 4 triangles.

   - 4 rectangles 6" by 8" for the large sections in the second block.

- ## Piecing

1. Using your preferred method of FPP, make the (4) HST Squares and the 4 Inner Squares

2. Using a 1/4" seam allowance, sew each row together. Press the seam in the direction of the arrows.

   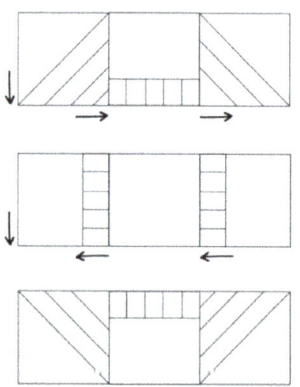

3. Layering the batting and backing, quilt and bind as desired.

Square Panel Star Quilt

Materials

- 6 square fabric panels, trimmed to 10 1/2" x 10 1/2"
- 3-6 fat quarters (or 3/4 yards) of coordinating fabric to make the stars
- 2 3/4 yards of background fabric
- 3 1/2 yards of fabric for the back of the quilt (or enough fabric to piece together a 62" x 72" quilt back)
- a piece of quilt batting at least 62" x 72"
- 1/2 yard of binding fabric (6-7 binding strips)

- a rotary cutter, acrylic ruler, and mat
- sewing machine
- thread (I suggest thread matching the background fabric)
- ironing board and iron
- a pencil or fabric marking pen

Instructions

• Cutting

From six different coordinating fabrics , cut:

- 4 squares 5 7/8" x 5 7/8"

From the background fabric, cut:

- 6 squares 11 1/4" x 11 1/4"
- 2 rectangles 10 1/2" x 20 1/2"
- 2 rectangles 5 1/2" x 35 1/2"
- 8 rectangles 5 1/2" x 10 1/2"
- 2 squares 5 1/2" x 5 1/2"
- 6 strips 4" x 42" (for the border)

• Make Four Flying Geese Units for Each Star

Use a 1/4" (or scant 1/4") seam allowance throughout this quilt pattern.

1. Use the pencil or fabric marking pen to draw a diagonal line across the wrong side of four 5 7/8" print fabric squares for a star.

2. Place two 5 7/8" squares right sides together on a 11 1/4" background fabric square, aligned with opposite corners.

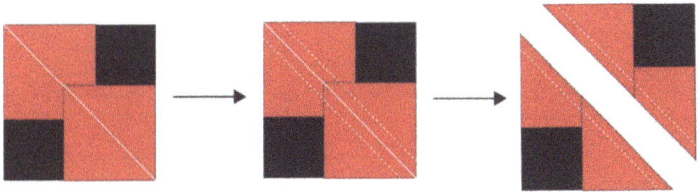

3. Sew 1/4" away from the drawn line on either side. Cut the piece apart along the line. Fold the small triangles up and press.

4. Place another 5 7/8" square right side down on each piece, aligned with the remaining corner as shown. Stitch 1/4" away from the drawn line on either side.

5. Cut apart the pieces along the line. Fold back the triangles and press to make 4 flying geese units. Press. Trim the flying geese units to 5 1/2" x 10 1/2".

6. Make 4 matching flying geese that will be sewn around a square fabric panel piece to make a sawtooth star.

7. Then repeat this step with the 5 other fabrics, making a total of 24 flying geese units, 4 to go around each fabric panel piece.

- **Sew the Flying Geese and Other Fabric Pieces into Rows**

  1 Arrange the flying geese pieces and all of the remaining background fabric pieces (except the border strips) on a quilt design wall. Make 7 rows as shown.

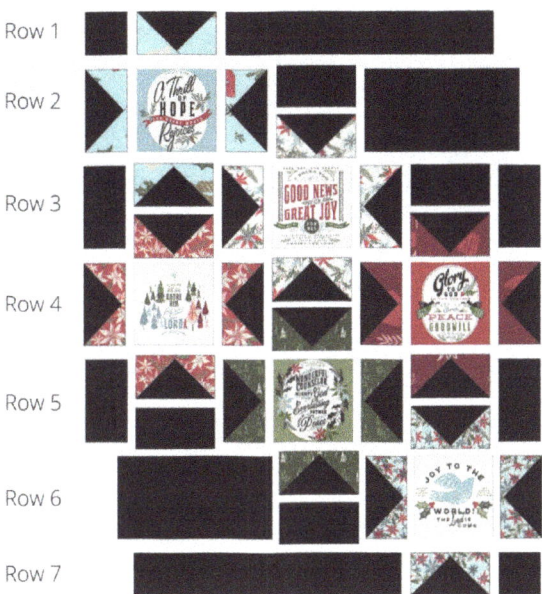

  2 Within each row, there are flying geese units that must be sewn to fabric rectangles or to other flying geese units before you can assemble each row.

  3 Sew pieces in each row together.

  4 Sew the seven rows together to make the quilt top.

- **Measure and Sew the Border Pieces**

Sew all the 4" strips of background fabric together to make one long strip. The expected length of the side border pieces is 60 1/2".

- **Finishing the Quilt**

1. Cut or piece together a piece of quilt backing fabric at least 62" x 72". The batting should be the same size as the quilt back. Make a quilt sandwich with the backing, batting, and top.

2. Baste together

3. Quilt as desired.

4. Trim and square up the quilt, removing extra backing and batting. Cut the needed amount of binding strips.

Merry Stars Quilt

Materials

- 1 1/2 yards Pixie Dot White
- 1 yard Santa's Crew Wintergreen
- 1 yardLinear Argyle Red
- 1/4 yard Christmas Trees Dk Wintergreen
- 1/2 yard Linear Argyle Med Wintergreen
- 1/4 yard Christmas Pets Gray
- 1/2 yard Snowflake Stripe White
- 1/3 yard Christmas Pets Pale Wintergreen
- 1/3 yard Christmas Trees Gray
- 1 yard Snowflake Stripe Red (for binding and in piano keys border)
- plus 4 yards of fabric for the backing

Instructions

• Cutting

Following the chart bellow:

Merry Stars Cutting Chart:

Fabric:	Placement:	Cut:	also cut:
Pixie Dot White	background of 48" star	1 square - 25 1/4"	4 squares - 12 1/2"
	corner squares behind appliqué	4 squares - 10"	
Santa's Crew Wintergreen	points of the 48" star	4 squares - 12 7/8"	
Linear Argyle Red	background of 24" star	1 square - 13 1/4"	4 squares - 6 1/2"
Christmas Trees Dk Wintergreen	points of the 24" star	4 squares - 6 7/8"	
Linear Argyle Med Wintergreen	background of the 12" star	1 square - 7 1/4"	4 squares - 3 1/2"
Christmas Pets Pale Gray	points of the 12" star	4 squares - 3 7/8"	
Snowflake Stripe White	background of the 6" star	1 square - 4 1/4"	4 squares - 2"
Linear Argyle Red	points of the 6" star	4 squares - 2 3/8"	
Fussy cut elf from Santa's Crew fabric	center of the 6" star	1 square 3 1/2"	
6 different fabrics: • Linear Argyle Red • Snowflake Stripe Red • Christmas Trees Dk Wintergreen • Santa's Crew Wintergreen • Christmas Pets Pale Wintergreen • Snowflake Stripe White	piano keys border	4 strips from each fabric: 2 1/2" x width of fabric (24 strips total)	
Linear Argyle Med Wintergreen	holly leaves	8 leaves from appliqué template	
Linear Argyle Red	berries	12 berries from appliqué template	

- **Sew the first Star Block**

Sew the first (6") star block with a cute 3 1/2" fussy cut elf in the center. After that, each star block will become the center of the next larger one.

The points and background of each star are formed from 4 flying geese units and 4 corner squares. After all your cutting is done, start by making the first 4 flying geese:

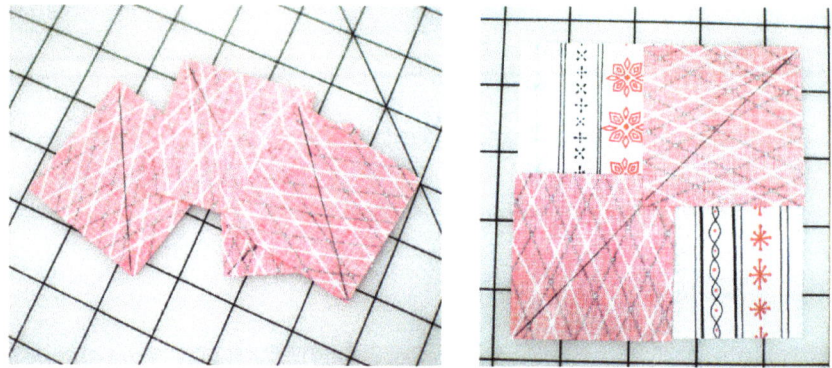

- **Make 4 flying geese units from 5 squares**

1. Draw a diagonal line across the back of the 2 3/8" squares that will make the points of the star. Pin 2 squares to opposite corners of the 4 1/4" background fabric square

2. Sew 1/4" away from either side of the lines, diagonally across the square. Then cut along the drawn lines.

3. Sew the first (6") star block with a cute 3 1/2" fussy cut elf in the center. After that, each star block will become the center of the next larger one.

4. Cut along the line again and you've got 4 flying geese units!

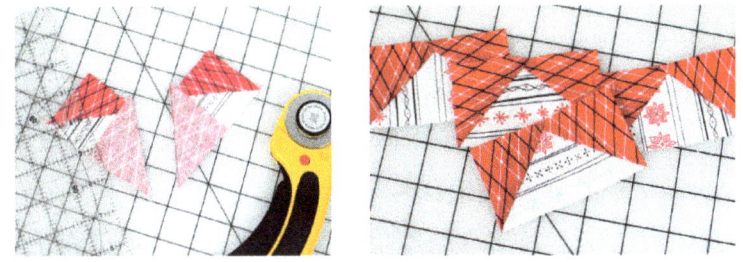

5. Arrange the flying geese units with the 3 1/2" center square and the 2" background corner square units as shown above left. Stitch together in three rows first. Then sew the rows together to make the block.

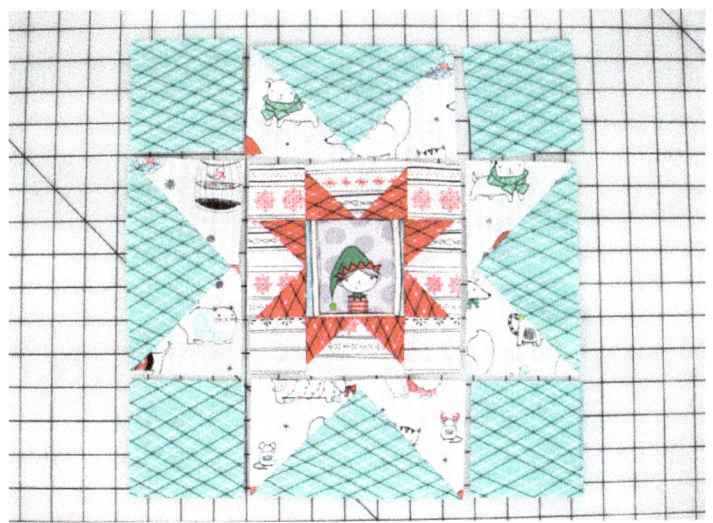

- **Continue the pattern of variable stars**

1. Use the four 3 7/8" and the 7 1/4" squares to make flying geese units for the 12" star. Assemble together with the first star block and the 3 1/2" background corner squares. Stitch.

2. Use the four 6 7/8" and the 13 1/4" squares to make flying geese units for the 24" star. Assemble together with the second star block and the 6 1/2" background corner squares. Stitch.

3. Use the four 12 7/8" and the 25 1/4" squares to make flying geese units for the 48" star. Assemble together with the first star block and the 12 1/2" background corner squares. Stitch.

- **Make the border**

1. Trace the Holly & Berries pattern on to the back of the Heat n Bond Lite to make 8 holly leaves and 12 berries. Fuse 2 leaves and three berries to a 10" corner square piece as shown above right. Stitch around the shapes as desired.

2. Divide the twenty-four 2 1/2" strips into 4 sets, each with 6 strips

3. Sew 6 strips together to make a strip set that is approximately 12 1/2" x 42".

4. Cut off the selvages and subcut the strip set into 4 pieces that are each 10" wide.

5. Turn the strips and sew the 4 pieces together to make a piano keys border piece that is 10" x 48 1/2".

6. Arrange the center star block, the 4 corner blocks, and the border pieces as shown above and sew together.

7. Quilt and bind as desired

Winter Watch Quilt

Materials

- the fabric panel
- 1 yard of coordinating fabric for the stars and stripes (mine is red)
- 1 yard of background fabric
- 3 1/4 yards of fabric for the back of the quilt (or enough fabric to piece together a 57" x 63" quilt back)
- a piece of quilt batting at least 57" x 63"
- 1/2 yard of binding fabric (6 binding strips)

- a rotary cutter, acrylic ruler, and mat
- sewing machine
- thread (I suggest thread matching the background fabric)
- ironing board and iron
- pencil or fabric marking pen

Instructions

• Cutting

First, trim off any fabric around the printed image on your fabric panel and square it up.

33"

41"

From the darker coordinating fabric, cut:

- 8 strips 2 1/2" x WOF (width of fabric)
- 28 squares 2 7/8" x 2 7/8"

From the background fabric, cut:

- 8 strips 2 1/2" x WOF
- 4 squares 5 1/4" x 5 1/4"
- 4 squares 3 3/8" x 3 3/8"
- 4 squares 2 7/8" x 2 7/8"
- 8 squares 2 1/2" x 2 1/2"

• Make the Centers of the Star Blocks

Use a 1/4" (or scant 1/4") seam allowance throughout this quilt pattern.

1 Cut 8 of the darker fabric 2 7/8" squares in half diagonally. You will need 4 triangles for the center of each star.

2 Mark a center line across each background fabric 3 3/8" square.

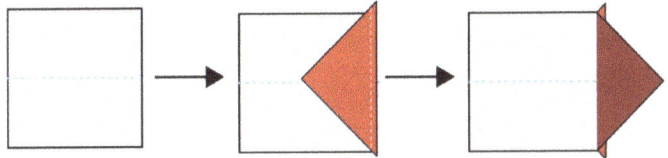

3 Sew a darker fabric triangle to one side of the square, using the center line you marked

4 Then sew another darker fabric triangle to the other side of the square. Press the points of the triangle outward.

5 Sew two more darker fabric triangles to the top and bottom edges of the square.

Press the block and trim away the dog ears and any extra fabric to make the block 4 1/2" square. Repeat to make 4 pieces.

- **Make 16 Flying Geese Units**

  1. Use the pencil or fabric marking pen to draw a diagonal line across the wrong side of 16 of the remaining 2 7/8" darker fabric squares.

  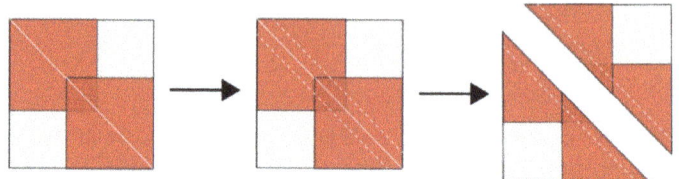

  2. Place two 2 7/8" squares right sides together on a 5 1/4" background fabric square, aligned with opposite corners.

  3. Sew 1/4" away from the drawn line on either side. Cut the piece apart along the line. Fold the small triangles up and press.

  4. Place another 2 7/8" square right side down on each piece, aligned with the remaining corner as shown. Stitch 1/4" away from the drawn line on either side.

  5. Cut apart the pieces along the line. Fold back the triangles and press to make 4 flying geese units. Press. Trim the flying geese units to 2 1/2" x 4 1/2".

  Repeat to make 16 pieces.

- **Make 8 Half Square Triangles (HST's)**

1. Use the pencil or fabric marking pen to draw a diagonal line across the wrong side of all of the 2 7/8" background fabric squares.

2. Sew 1/4" away from the cutting line on on both sides of the line.

3. Cut each piece in half diagonally along the line. Open and press to make 2 half square triangles (HST units). Press. Trim each HST to 2 1/2" square. Repeat to make 8 HST units.

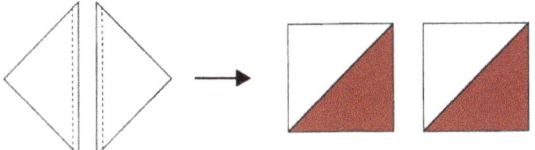

- **Make 4 Sawtooth Star Blocks**

1. Arrange the following pieces as shown to make a Sawtooth Star Block:

   - 1 center piece
   - 4 flying feese units
   - 2 half square triangle units
   - 2 background fabric squares 2 1/2" x 2 1/2"

2. Sew together in 3 rows.

3. Sew the rows together to make the block.

- **Make the Striped Border Pieces**

1. Cut 4 darker fabric strips that are 2 1/2" wide.

2. Cut 4 background fabric strips that are 2 1/2" wide.

3. Sew these strips together in 2 sets. Each set should have 4 strips in an alternating pattern. Press.

4. Cut and piece 4 dark and 4 background 2½" strips to match the panel's short side. Sew into 2 sets of alternating strips.

5. Sew the Sawtooth Star Blocks to the ends of the shorter strip sets. Make two.

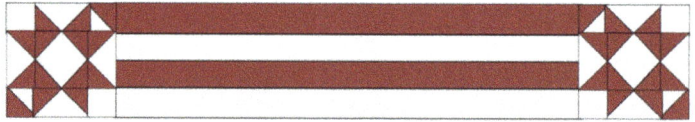

- **Assemble the Easy Panel Quilt**

1. Sew the longer strip sets to the longer edges of the fabric panel.

2. Sew the shorter strip sets with the star blocks on the ends to the shorter edges of the fabric panel.

3. Quilt as desired

Winter Tree Quilt

Materials

- 1 yard of light green fabric for the large tree blocks
- 5/8 yard of pink fabric for 6 small tree blocks
- 5/8 yard of turquoise fabric for 7 small tree blocks
- 3 1/2 yards of background fabric
- a rotary cutter, acrylic ruler, and mat
- sewing machine
- thread (I suggest thread matching the background fabric)
- ironing board and iron
- pencil or fabric marking pen

- 4 yards of backing fabric (or enough to piece together a 75" x 65" quilt back)
- a piece of quilt batting at least 65" x 75"
- 1/2–5/8 yard of binding fabric (7–8 binding strips)

Instructions

- ## Cutting

From the light green fabric (for the large trees), cut:

- 3 squares 9 1/4" x 9 1/4"
- 3 squares 11 1/4 x 11 1/4"
- 3 squares 13 1/4" x 13 1/4"

From the pink fabric (for 6 small trees), cut:

- 2 squares 7 1/4" x 7 1/4"
- 2 squares 9 1/4" x 9 1/4"
- 2 squares 11 1/4 x 11 1/4"

From the turquoise fabric (for 7 small trees), cut:

- 2 squares 7 1/4" x 7 1/4"
- 2 squares 9 1/4" x 9 1/4"
- 2 squares 11 1/4 x 11 1/4"

From the dark gray background fabric, cut:

- 36 squares 4 7/8" x 4 7/8"
- 24 rectangles 4 1/2" x 1 1/2"
- 24 rectangles 4 1/2" x 2 1/2"
- 39 squares 3 7/8" x 3 7/8"
- 26 rectangles 3 1/2" x 1 1/2"
- 26 rectangles 3 1/2" x 2 1/2"
- 13 strips 2 1/2" x 9 1/2"
- 13 strips 3 1/2" x 12 1/2"
- 9 strips 2 1/2" x 42" (for the sashing)
- 4 strips 2 1/2" x 42" (for the side borders)

- **Sub-Cutting**

1. Cut all of the 4 7/8" squares and 3 7/8" squares in half diagonally to make half square triangles.

2. Cut the light green 9 1/4" squares in half diagonally twice to make quarter square triangles that are 9 1/4" wide at the bottom. (12)

3. Make 12 trapezoids that are 11 1/4" wide at the bottom and 4 1/2" tall.

4. Make 12 trapezoids that are 13 1/4" wide at the bottom and 4 1/2" tall.

5. Make 6 pink trapezoids that are 9 1/4" wide at the bottom and 3 1/2" tall.

6. Make 6 pink trapezoids that are 11 1/4" wide at the bottom and 3 1/2" tall.

 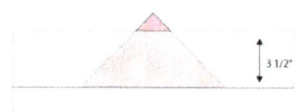 

7. Make 7 turquoise trapezoids that are 9 1/4" wide at the bottom and 3 1/2" tall.

8. Make 7 turquoise trapezoids that are 11 1/4" wide at the bottom and 3 1/2" tall.

- **Sew the Large Tree Blocks**

1. Sew two of the larger (4 7/8") half square triangles to the sides of a light green quarter square triangle that is 9 1/4" wide at the bottom. Press and trim to 4 1/2" x 8 1/2". Make 12.

2. Sew two of the larger (4 7/8") half square triangles to the sides of a light green trapezoid that is 11 1/4" wide at the bottom. Press and trim to 4 1/2" x 10 1/2". Make 12.

3. Sew two of the larger (4 7/8") half square triangles to the sides of a light green trapezoid that is 13 1/4" wide at the bottom. Press and trim to 4 1/2" x 12 1/2". Make 12.

4. Sew two 4 1/2" x 2 1/2" rectangles to the sides of a 4 1/2" x 8 1/2" piece to make a 4 1/2" x 12 1/2" piece. Press. Make 12.

5. Sew two 4 1/2" x 1 1/2" rectangles to the sides of a 4 1/2" x 10 1/2" piece to make a 4 1/2" x 12 1/2" piece. Press. Make 12.

6. Sew three different 4 1/2" x 12 1/2" pieces together to make a 12 1/2" x 12 1/2" tree block as shown above. Press. Make 12 tree blocks.

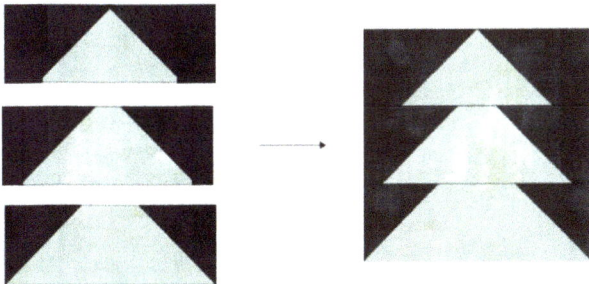

• Sew the Small Trees

Sew the same way as The Big ones

Make 6 pink trees and 7 turquoise trees.

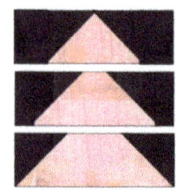 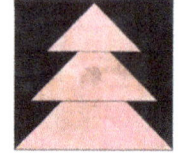

Sew a 2 1/2" x 9 1/2" background fabric strip to the left (right) side of a tree piece. Press. Sew a 3 1/2" x 12 1/2" background fabric strip to the bottom of the piece.

- Make 4 pink right sided small tree blocks.
- Make 3 turquoise right sided small tree blocks.
- Make 2 pink left sided small tree blocks.
- Make 4 turquoise left sided small tree blocks.

• Assemble the Winter Tree Quilt

1. Arrange the 25 quilt blocks in an alternating pattern on a large table

2. Sew the blocks together to make 5 rows.

3. Piece together 2 1/2" x 42" background fabric strips to make 6 sashing rows that are 2 1/2" x 60 1/2".

4. Quilts as Desired

Conclusion

As we close the final chapter of **Christmas Quilting: Patterns to Spark Holiday Cheer**, we hope this guide has done more than teach techniques—it has inspired joy, creativity, and connection. Each stitch you've made brings with it the warmth of tradition and the beauty of handmade expression, especially meaningful during the holiday season.

Quilting is more than a craft—it's a way to tell stories, preserve memories, and create something lasting. Whether you've made a festive wall hanging, a cozy throw, or a special gift, your work carries the love and care that make Christmas truly magical. These quilts will warm more than homes; they will warm hearts for years to come.

We encourage you to make these patterns your own—add your personal flair, incorporate family history, or start new traditions. Let your creativity continue to shine beyond these pages.

Thank you for allowing us to be part of your holiday journey. May your quilts bring comfort, your holidays sparkle with joy, and your hands stay busy with inspiration.

Merry Christmas, and happy quilting!

www.ingramcontent.com/pod-product-compliance
Ingram Content Group UK Ltd.
Pitfield, Milton Keynes, MK11 3LW, UK
UKHW020805161025
8418UKWH00022B/477